D1217697

HOUSTON PUBLIC LIBRARY

KING WILLIAM THE WANDERER.

The Hyperion Library of World Literature

HYPERION PRESS, INC.
Westport, Connecticut

KING WILLIAM THE WANDERER,
AN OLD BRITISH SAGA, FROM
OLD FRENCH VERSIONS.

BY

W. G. COLLINGWOOD.

PRINTED BY THE LANTHORN
PRESS, AND PUBLISHED IN LONDON
BY S. C. BROWN LANGHAM & CO.,
LTD., 47, GREAT RUSSELL STREET,
W.C., 1904.

R0140049913
HUM

HOUSTON PUBLIC LIBRARY

Published in 1904 by S. C. Brown Langham & Company, Ltd.
Hyperion reprint edition 1978
Library of Congress Catalog Number 76-48418
ISBN 0-88355-534-4
Printed in the United States of America

Library of Congress Cataloging in Publication Data
Chrestien de Troyes, 12th cent.
    King William the Wanderer.

    (The Hyperion library of world literature)
    Translation of the poem by Chrestien de Troyes and
Le dit de Guillaume d'Angleterre. Cf. BM.
    Reprint of the 1904 ed. published by S. C. Brown
Langham, London.
    I. Title.
PQ 1447.E5C58 1978 843'.1 76-48418
ISBN 0-88355-534-4

Chrestien of Troyes, mentioned on the opposite page, was the most famous French poet of the twelfth century, author of Arthurian romances taken from Welsh sources. He says that this tale was told him by a friend named "Rogiers li Cointes," *Roger the Charming*, and that it is a true story which can be found at "Saint Esmoing" (*Bury St. Edmunds*, I suppose) in the histories of England. Another, perhaps earlier, version was printed with Chrestien's poem by Francisque Michel in "Chroniques Anglo-Normands" (Rouen, 1840). In this rendering I have combined the two versions, supplying from the one what seemed lacking in the other.

KING WILLIAM THE WANDERER.

CHAPTER I.

OF KING WILLIAM AND GRATIANA HIS QUEEN.

THE story tells how there was once a king who lived in England, and his name was king William. He was a good and God-fearing man, most charitable and most humble. Holy church he always honoured, and the poor were never driven from the door of his hall. So he ruled his land in peace, and the people loved him.

This king William took to wife a fair and good maiden, and loved her dearly, as you may well believe, and she loved him as much again, or even more. She was a king's daughter, but the old story gives no name to her father; and — says its ancient author, Chrestien of Troyes — we tell no idle tales, nor set down a word above what is written. Her name was Gratiana, and her nature was like her name — gracious in word and deed. If the king served his lord the King of Paradise, no less did she; and all her heart she put into the service of God. If the king was

5

kind and humble, so was the queen. Never a morning did he fail to rise early and hear matins, and every morning she went with him to the minster. They lived a holy life, and to all poor members of the body of Christ they showed most perfect love and charity.

So for six years they lived together in peace and piety, and yet that pretty queen had no children. The people at last began to murmur because their was no heir to the kingdom, and some said it was high time for the king to take another wife and make his throne steadfast, for if he died, what wars and tumults would come about, when there was no son to take his father's place !

But when the king heard these murmurs he was greatly grieved, and angered too. He swore before them all that he would never do such a thing. He loved his lady too dearly and too loyally to think of parting from her—no, not until the end of the world.

Thereupon trouble began to break out in the realm, though it did not last for long, because, by God's grace, in the seventh year came the promise of an heir. Folk were fain of that, but

6

you shall see how their gladness endured only for a little while, and how sore was the sorrow that fell upon England afterwards.

As time went on, the queen grew sick and ailing. The king thought no care and comfort too good for her, and watched over her as one who had nothing dearer in life.

One morning early, at the hour when they used to rise and go to matins, the bells began to ring. But he saw that she was not strong enough to stir from her bed.

" Sweetheart," said he, " I must away to church, but for God's sake bide thou quiet and never think of coming with me. It would be folly, and if harm happened, indeed and truly— under God—I should go out of my mind."

"Dear my lord," she answered, " here I stay Thy will and my will are always at one."

So the king went to church, and the sweet lady lay there in her bed. But she never slept. She said her prayers over and over until her dear man should come back again : and the book says that she was very glad to see him.

7

CHAPTER II.

HOW A VOICE BADE HIM GO FORTH INTO THE WIDE WORLD.

ONCE, on a dark morning before dawn, he woke up as he used, a little earlier than the hour of matins, and lay wondering why he heard no bells ring. Suddenly there was a peal of thunder, and as he raised his head the room was all ablaze with light. It blinded him, and a Voice seemed to come down from the very heaven, saying :—

"O great has been thy gladness, and the glee thou hast cherished ;
But mind thee and mark. Ere the moon's fulfilling
Thy life and thy love shall be lost thee for ever
So thou heed not Him whom the heavens adore.
Go now in the guiding of God Almighty
And wander awide in the world before thee.
See no man know it, and nought bewray it
Till a score of summers be spent, and four.
Let be thy bliss, for thy bane is in it,
To reap the riches of the realm of glory,
Then forth and fear not, nor faint in going,
When Christ bids thee carry the cross that He bore."

Then the Voice ended, and the vision faded as suddenly as it had come. All in wonderment, the king donned his clothes and drew on his shoes, and bade folk run for his confessor there

8

and then. While they walked to the minster he told what the Voice had said, and how the light had burst into his chamber. The priest, a wise and loyal man, listened long to him.

"Lord king," he said at last, "as touching this vision, I cannot tell whence it has come. Maybe it is an evil dream from the devil. Never leave the realm unfriended for such a thing. Maybe again it is because of sin. This or that may have been taken unrighteously. My counsel is to make proclamation forthwith that if man or woman have claim upon thee or on thy father (whom God assoil) they shall be fully satisfied. Keep nothing back that is another's, and be clear of every charge. Without doubt such a vision has not come for nought."

"That I will," said the king, whose only thought was to be right with God : and the very morning he sent criers throughout his realm and bade come to his court all to whom he or his father might owe anything. Folk came in flocks, and many with idle tales; but of all who could show just cause there was not one, gentle or simple, who did not carry away the uttermost farthing. Furthermore he gave large

9

and noble gifts to poor abbeys and to the servants of God. So all men prayed for that king.

But the good Lord, who tries the hearts of His people, sent once more to him. While he lay in bed, just at the hour when he had seen it before, he saw the brightness and heard the Voice. It called him by name, saying : —

> " O sore shall be thy sorrow, if thou scorn the commandment !
> O foolish and faithless, wouldst thou fall in thine error ?
> When the bidding of the Blessed One has beckoned, wouldst thou tarry ?
> I leave thee ; but look to it, and linger no more."

Mightily troubled and afraid, the king rose in haste, doubting of what he had seen and heard. He went straight to church, and when matins had been sung he called the chaplain aside, that same confessor of whom we have heard, and told him in what guise the Voice had come again, to bid him in the name of God go forth and be a wanderer in the wide world. " And most grievously it threatened me," said he, " if I refrain."

When the confessor heard that word he said " Never fear, my lord ; patience, and never fear ! Dear my lord, it is well known Holy Writ bids a man leave house and lands, wife and children, to win the bliss no eye hath seen : but, my gracious king, one boon I beg. Seeing we cannot tell whether this be an idle dream or no, wait till the Voice return, before leaving thy royal estate. It is but reason. If the Voice come a third time, then I shall deem it of God, and it will be right to go forth, for every man of us must do His behest. But in the meanwhile cast aside all this world's goods; love God alone and hold everything else in contempt. Scatter abroad without grudging all thy gold and silver ; give it to the poor, and to abbeys which are God's houses, and to churches, for on them most worthily are alms bestowed. You have copes and rings, coats and mantles, robes and coverlets, falcons and hawks, chargers and palfreys ; give away in one gift all the goods that are left, even to a chestnut's worth,—to the value of a straw from the thatch, but only the clothes ye stand in : and God in His own good time shall render it an hundredfold, yea, twice an hundredfold shall be laid up in heaven for recompense."

Now this could not be gainsaid, and that the king knew. So he made answer, " Well, father, so be it. But as thy hope is in God, hide this matter ; reveal never a word of it, but hold it as a thing under seal of confession."

"May I never reach forgiveness, lord king, if tongue of mine betray my trust."

Long that day after matins ended the king abode on his knees, praying that if it were God's will to send him forth the Voice might come once more, and then he would willingly and joyfully go whither he was bidden. Then he came back to his chamber and found his wife lying quiet in her bed, for she had fallen asleep at break of dawn. All day he was heavy with thought, but never forgot his errand. He bade men set out before him all his treasure, and sent for abbots and priors of needy struggling houses, and abbesses and prioresses poor and in want, and gladdened their hearts, giving them all his goods for the love of God. Also the queen, for she was one with him in everything, gave up her furs of grey and ermine, and her rings and jewels; keeping back nothing worth a rag of her wimple.

Throughout the day they were busy with that work until the evening, and then in the night they lay long wakeful, each unknown to the other sleepless with care and thought. At the last they

fell into a slumber, and then came the messenger
from Paradise, calling again upon the king and
saying : —

"Thou fool ! will thou fail then ?   Go forth of thy kingdom
Unnamed and unknown of noble or simple.
What if thirsting or hunger thou thole, aye or thraldom,
So God will to grant thee His guerdon therefor ? "

CHAPTER III

HOW THE QUEEN WOULD NOT LET HIM GO ALONE.

THE king crept forth from his bed, silent and full of care, all mother-naked as he was—for then-a-days folk slept so—and blessed himself, and donned the plainest garment he could find in the room. He took neither gold nor silver, but only girded his sword to him, and gave one kiss to the crosslet hilt. He thought the queen was fast asleep, and he sighed, saying in a low voice—" Sweetheart, I must away ! Sweet and true friend, I shall never see thee again, nor the child for whom I have hoped."

But the queen heard, and her heart ached for him. She made as though she were just awaking, and asked whither he went.

"Lady, I am going to matins ; hark how the bells ring ! "

" Ah, king," said the queen, " Your love would play me false ; but mine is true, and shall never fail you ! "

14

Then she fell at his feet, crying,—"Dear lord, for the sake of God who loves no lies, indeed and truly I have heard the Voice that has come these three times. You think to leave me ; but nay ! For I will never leave you, so long as I live. Go forth into the wide world if it must be, but not without me ! "

"For God's sake, speak low, sweetheart ! If they hear, if folk know I am bound on such a journey, thy will never let me out of their hands for all I could do."

Again, and the third and fourth time, he begged and prayed her to let him go in peace and tell no one, nor even send to seek him.

"King," she answered, "this is folly. I could not bide in life alone. We two have been lovers together so long, that it is my place to bear your trials. We have had joy and wealth, honour and ease together ; let us share sorrow, poverty, shame and toil. Far more than I can say I long to be helpmate in your grief as I have been in your gladness."

He was an English king ; he was no churlish carle. He kissed the queen with tears and sobs, and at last he said, " But, sweetheart, if I take

15

thee with me, what of the hope of an heir that is
to be ?   For a hundred thousand byzant marks
I would not have thee come to harm in yonder
woodlands and wilds.   Where should we find
folk to serve, meat and drink for a queen-mother,
nurse for the child ?   Short would be thy life,
and nothing but sorrow and suffering.   If thou
fear not for thyself, if nothing daunts thee, have
pity on the babe that is to be.   Give him at least
the chance to live.   If we let him die through
heedlessness, it will be thine own death-blow ;
and then what should I do ?   The death of you
twain would kill me too, and we should all be lost
for one alone.   Far better bide here in hall, with
gold to spend, and myrrh to scent the baby's bed ;
lie soft, and nurse the king that is coming.   What
says the saying ? — ' Folk that will not follow rede
find themselves in woeful need ' : — and if I give
ill counsel now, never believe me again ! "

   To which she only answered, " But if I stay,
be sure the grief will kill me outright !   You
reason well, but there is One that says ' They that
put their trust in Me shall never be confounded.'
Nay, I will not leave you, never !   God will not
forget you, nor will he forget me, nor the child

that shall be ours. The same bidding has come to both of us, and He will keep both of us in obeying it."

So at last the king must needs yield, against his better counsel, and they set out on their way together.

CHAPTER IV.

HOW THEY STOLE AWAY.

NOW they dared not open the door of their chamber, for fear their people might hear them and be aware of their going. But in that room there were windows. Through one of them the king went first, and lifted down the queen tenderly and lovingly, and then led her by the hand through the long garden—for there was no moon and the night was dark before the dawn—and so out of a little gate which he knew well.

Just as day was breaking they reached a great wood and hid themselves within it, in mighty fear lest anyone should spy them. He had his sword ; nothing else they took away with them but a good heart, undaunted and undivided.

In that forest there were neither roads nor paths, for the people of the land never travelled through it whether outward or homeward ; no way led beyond it. So they fled into the thickest of the wood and wandered about for a long while. It was hard faring, but they took comfort, knowing that whom God inspires and leads with His light He gladdens with His joy, and all things are lovely to those who feel His love.

In the morning when people awoke they wondered why the king was not astir — he who was used to be astir so early. When the sun was high they began to whisper that he must be sick, though little they knew what cause there was for sorrow.

They sat outside, waiting a weary while, until noon was passed. Then they tried the door, and found it barred. They held them still and listened long. Then they called at the door and knocked, and in the end they beat so hard on plank and panel that they broke it in.

Who but wondered then to find neither king nor queen? The window stood open and they were gone. Their folk sought high and low, but never found them.

So the grooms and the kitchen knaves ransacked the chamber; they burst open kists and arks and made havoc of the house, laying hands on all they could find.* But little they got of all

---

*This ransacking of the palace at the death of a king (polotasvarf) was the ancient right belonging to the Varangian guard of the Greek Emperors at Constantinople. The incident, which is essential to the plot of the story, takes us back to the Viking age.

they hoped ; little there was to find where all had been given away. Only a young lad spied under the bed an ivory horn which, the story says, the king used to carry when he went hunting in the woods ; and he took it home and kept it safe. You shall see how it stood him in good stead many a year afterward.

It was not long before the news flew about that the king was gone. The whole realm was troubled ; and when they heard that the queen was gone too, it was a loss that fell upon all. They made no delay, but searched by land and sea, in every part but just where the wanderers were hidden.

Now these two roamed about in the pathless forest and lived like savage folk on acorns and grass and wild fruits. They ate blackberries and raspberries, nuts and crab-apples, sloes and ramps, anything they could find, and drank the rain of heaven for want of better drink. But they took everything in good part. The king began to grow brown in the sun and lean with hunger ; his gown was well nigh torn to tatters ; but God's especial goodness kept the queen in all her beauty.

20

Well, they were a month in this forest, wandering on from day to day and never finding path nor track until at last one morning they were out of the wood, and there was the sea !*

They found a cave in the rocks and crept into it for a lodging that night. It was the best home they could find, a house of little ease, hard bed and cold kitchen. But the queen was so wearied out that if she slept sound it was no wonder. And yet she was very sick and like to die, and before she slept she called the king to her and taking a ring from her finger she sighed and said " Keep this ring in remembrance of me."

" That will I," said he, " by all the faith I owe."

But little he knew how many a day should pass before he could put that ring upon her finger again.

---

*The French book calls this place " Gernemue," that is, *Yarmouth*.

CHAPTER V.

HOW THE QUEEN WAS CARRIED OFF BY SEA-FARERS.

YONDER in the cave by the sea-shore were born two fair boys to the king and queen of England. They had no nurse to wait on them, no bed to lie on, no clothes for their swaddling. But what a man could do, that the king did, in all humility and sweetness, following the bidding of the queen for every little service, without disdain or displeasure ; and a right good servant he made. He bethought him how he could hap the babies—they were so dear to him. Drawing his sword he slit off the two skirts of his gown, and wrapped one in each piece. Then he sat there with the queen's head on his knees, kind and true and tender, until she should find rest ; and in that manner she slumbered until morning was come.

But in the morning when she awoke, " Ah, dear lord ! " she cried, " I am so hungered that I am well nigh out of my wits. I shall die if I may not have something to eat, and that at once ! "

22

What could the king do but call upon the mercy of God ?

Then she went on—for she was like one distraught—"At the least, if I can have neither bread nor flesh, give me one of those babes to eat ! "

He started up full of pity for her, and could not think what to do, until it came to him that if she must have flesh of man to eat—why, there was his. Drawing his sword he made as he would cut the brawn of his thigh to give her. But she cried, " For God's sake, dear lord, nay ! " —and caught him by the hand saying, " I shall indeed go mad if I see thee cut thyself. God forbid teeth of mine should eat flesh of thine ! "

" Alas, sweetheart, " said he in bitter anguish, " How else can I lay thy hunger. Better eat all the flesh from my bones, if I save my little son from death. The Lord maybe might heal my wound and give me back my strength, but never the life of that little child. Nay, He knows if ye did such a thing as eat your own babe, you would die yourself of sorrow and shame."

Then she burst into bitter tears, and it seemed as though her hunger were quenched for the pity of it.

" I will bear my pain," she said, " and my hunger as well as I can ; but go and look for food. Cast about for folk who may give alms for the love of God. It kills me to wait, but I will wait patiently."

He promised her that he would be back as soon as ever he could, and went out of the cave to look for bread. In a while he came to a harbourage of the sea, and there he found a company of chapman busied in unloading their ship, laughing and shouting merrily. He went up to them, but this king was so poverty-stricken and naked that he seemed like the lowest gangrel knave that tramps the roads.

He bowed humbly and begged them to hear him. " Kind lords, may God be good to you and give you increase. If you have a morsel of meat to spare give me to eat, and God render it you, and grant you safe wayfaring and great gains ! "

One of them, an evil carle, cried roughly, " Look you, lordings, at yon gangrel knave ! Stout and sturdy as a bull, and yet he goes begging his bread. Out ! Out ! rascal, before we thrash thee and duck thee, mark, to pay for this game ! "

"Hold!" cried another, who was the wiser man. "Never heat thyself for it: leave the poor beggar alone. Why stir a quarrel with him? 'Fools and knaves must live as they are able from the crumbs that fall from the goodman's table.' What need to make words about it? His trade is to beg up and down the world; this is not the first nor the last time; it is all the trade he knows."

"Ah, franklin," cried the king, "thanks! But indeed this is the first time, though if I must dree my weird it will not be the last."

"My word!" cried the evil carle with a loud voice, "Thy tongue was not left to pay thy last bill! Bygone bits are out of count!"

The king, in anguish of mind, answered humbly, "Lords, let it be as you please: but for God's sake have pity on me, or my wife will die, and truth it is, with her new-born babes. In a cave of the rocks they are lying, nigh dead of hunger, and she ready to eat her own children for want of meat."

"Ha, sir beggar! that is a lie!" said the first. "Here is a fine tale to tell folk! Never was such a devil in the flesh as a woman that

25

ate her own children. None ever did or ever will. And yet take us to thy place, if it is not too far."

"Maybe she is a pretty beggar-woman," said the other, "and that is how he hopes to get something out of us."

"Hark you now !" broke in the shipmaster. "On my faith, it would be a jest to see whether he tells the truth or no. Let us go with him, and if we find he lies, we'll thrash him till our staves break on his back."

So fifteen of them, bold fellows all, big and strong, took their staves, and had a mind to go : all swearing that if the beggar lied they would beat him so that his ribs would remember it for a year to come. The poor king led them straight to the cave where the fair queen lay with her two little babies.

"Lo there !" he said, "lords ; I am no liar. Yonder is my wife with her two little children."

They were so taken aback with her beauty that each made the sign of the cross over his face (for fear of witchcraft).

But soon the boldest of them cried out,

26

"Thou false knave, this is a hanging matter! Where didst find so fair a dame?"

"Friend, in very truth," he answered, "I am her husband."

"Ha, in very truth then, I was right when I called thee a liar. Must I knock out thy teeth before thy tongue tells truth? She is thy prisoner. Never think for to see the lady again : she has been too long in a beggar's hands ; she has been dragged up and down the country far too long. Finely wed is such a dame, tied to such a knave! Nay, no more of thy cringing and fooling ; speak truth! My word, there was no priest at this wedding! Wilt own where you stole her?"

"Ah, sir!" said the king, "say not so. Would God I were as easily quit of all the sins to my count. Robbery and ravishment I was never charged with. You do foul wrong to think so. What can I own when I know myself guiltless?"

"Devils take thee! So bonny a bird cannot own such a mate."

"Indeed and truly," the lady cried, "I am his lawful wedded wife!"

"More shame to thee for the lie. There is

27

nothing betwixt ye—Wedded, says she ? A bad
day it was when she fell into his hands, but there
is a better day coming. Take heart, dame, you
are free of the fellow now and henceforth. We
will carry you safe and sound into our ship and
keep you there like a lady—though "—he added,
seeing her terror and shame—" some folk never
know when they are well off. Any way, the fool
who brought you here has no more to do with
you. He can keep the two brats ; they will be
useful in his begging trade. Look you, sirrah,
take care of them and be good to them and it will
pay you well. As long as he sticks to them,
mates, he will never die of hunger and thirst."

At this the poor queen swooned away outright ; but when the king heard that word he
made no further semblance of courtesy, so wild
with anger and despair was he. His sword was
lying on the ground at his feet and he reached
out for it : but when they saw him laying hand
to hilt, one of them thrust him back, another
buffeted him in the face, a third snatched the
weapon, and a fourth bade fetch two stout poles
to make a litter and carry the lady away.

So a part of their company went into the

wood to cut two saplings. They made haste and tied them together with good cord, laid boughs and leafage and fern upon them for a bed, and then came back to the cave and carried off the lady upon it,—at their own will and pleasure, in her despite and his. He was in torment, but among them all he was held so fast that he could not withstand them, though he smote and struggled and maddened until they could hardly constrain him.

At last the shipmaster said it was sin and shame to belabour the poor wretch for nothing, and took out a red silk purse, saying, " My good fellow, hear reason. I will give thee five byzants of good red gold for to be still. When we are gone it will be no use following us. Take this, friend, byzants and purse and all, and then thou wilt have somewhat for thy living."

" Sir, I care nothing for your gold, and I scorn your gift. Keep your byzants—I will never have them ! "

" Knave, thou art too bold, and too foolish and proud. What, thou hast never a penny in the world ; wilt say nay to five pieces of gold ? Bye and bye this hot mood will cool ; see, I leave this here : when it likes thee, take it."

The shipmaster threw the purse toward the mouth of the cave ; so carelessly he flung it that it was caught in the branch of a tree and there it hung. They made no delay, but carried off the lady to their ship, and pushed out. Once afloat they hoisted the mast, up with the sail, and away they went : and he was left behind, wild with grief and rage. But all his lamentations and despair availed him nothing.

CHAPTER VI.

HOW THE KING LOST BOTH HIS CHILDREN THAT SAME DAY.

HE crept back to the cave, lamenting and maddening, and fell into thought what he might do next. If he stayed there, all the lords of the realm would seek him so diligently that they would find him in the end. At last he bethought him of two boats that were left on the beach, and said to himself that he would take one of them, and sail out on the high seas with his children, whithersoever God would lead him.

He took one of the babes, leaving the other in the cave, and went down to the sea-shore where the boat lay. He put the child on board and ran back to the cave where the other was sleeping. What did he find but a great grey wolf, with the child in its mouth! Wild with fear, and hardly aware what he was doing, he ran after the wolf. Far he ran and fast, but he could not reach it. His limbs failed, but still he struggled on. In the end, he lost sight of the beast, and all wearied out,

sank down upon a great rock and fell into slumber.

The story tells that this wolf, though it carried the child in its jaws, never harmed him at all, but ran forward till it came to a path where another company of chapmen were travelling. As soon as they saw it they shouted and hooted and threw sticks and stones at it, so that it dropped the prey upon the path, and fled.

The chapmen set out and ran to the place where the child lay. When they came there they took him up, and unwrapping the rag that swaddled him, lo and behold he was all safe, ay and smiling at them. They laughed loud again and made great mirth, for it seemed a rare miracle to find a baby unharmed out of the jaws of a wolf.

At last said one of them to the rest, " Sirs, I beg you let this child be mine. I warrant he shall be well looked after."

" Ye may have my share in him," said each ; and so the good fellow took up the bairn in his arms and swore he would reckon him his own son and make him a rich man too, unless ill hap stood in the way.

Now when this company of chapmen came to the sea-shore there was the other child lying in

one of their boats. He wailed out and cried lustily. They heard the noise and ran to see this new sight. One of them, a neighbour of the man who had taken the first child, fell straightway in love with the baby and would have him for his own.

"So be it," said his fellows, and when he vowed that he would hold the foundling as dear as any of his cousins or nephews if only it lived and did well, they all cried " Yours be it then ! It is a gift in good hands. We will all reckon it yours, and never a man shall gainsay ye ! "

So both the bairns got good foster-fathers. As yet nobody knew they were brothers, though everyone said how like they were ; they must have been born twins.

These chapmen took ship without further delay, and made a good voyage home to their land in Caithness. When they came among their own folk they bethought them of the children that they ought to be christened ; and at the christening they called one Wolfling, because he was taken from the wolf, and the other they·called Seaborn, because he was found in a boat on the sea.*

*The French books call one Louvet or Lovel, that is "little wolf," and the other Marins (Marinus), obviously French renderings of whatever were the names in the original story.

33

CHAPTER VII.

OF THE KING NOW LEFT DESOLATE.

AT last the poor king awoke from his swoon and slumber, in great sorrow and wrath. He cursed the chapmen who had carried off the queen, and then he cursed the wolf which had carried off the bairn. Then he bethought him of his last and only comfort, that he would run to his child who was left alone in the boat: —"For all the trouble I have had, maybe it shall be well with me yet, if only God grant I may recover him."

He dragged himself to the shore as well as he could, thinking to find the child he had left; but how his heart failed him when there was no child there ! All his grief was renewed and redoubled. It wanted but a little that he should have been quite out of his mind, and yet even in this plight he cursed not God. Nay, he found even somewhat to praise Him for, namely the purse which the chapman had given in alms. Now he would take it, and be thankful for small mercies.

34

So he crept back to the cave, where the purse was hanging from the bough of a tree, and climbed up to it. But just as he was reaching to take it an eagle swooped by, and saw the red thing hanging ; plucked it out of his hands and clapped its two wings in his face with such vehemence that it flung him to the ground.

He picked himself up and went on his knees saying, "Good Lord God, keep me from evil covetousness. In this one day have I lost both wife and children. Folly and wickedness it was to bring my lady with me. I am afflicted, yea, I am tormented beyond measure, dear Father Almighty ! But even as Thou didst let the enemy of hell tempt that good man they call Job to try him, so grant me patience and its perfect work, that evil make me not lose faith. I well believe that all this mischief has befallen me because I delayed so long to go forth when I was warned. Sweet King of Paradise, dearly have I paid for my sin ! My wife and children are lost,—God keep the realm of England in peace ! Its folk are brought low because of me. Oh marvellous and very marvellous it is that I live on, and my lady and her babes are lost. No sorer soul there is,

between this and the outer sea, than dwells in
my wretched body. Sweet Lady of Heaven, deign
to comfort me, and great charity wilt thou show.
The Lord gave me wife and children : the Lord
hath taken them away : blessed be the name of
the Lord ! "

Then he fell upon the cold earth and slept :
but God, who loved him, gave him the sight once
more, though only in a dream, of the dear wife
and little ones he had lost. He awoke ; the
vision was gone ; and yet it comforted him that
he had seen it.

He wandered forth by the seaside, not knowing whither he went, as grief led him this way or
that. He wandered hither and thither ; he sat
down in hopelessness, and started up again in
frenzy. He plunged into the wood and then
fought his way out of it. All day long he wandered thus, and when night came he could not
rest for the pain and the sorrow.

At last he lighted upon a green glade where
a party of chapmen were at their dinner. They
had made tables with their cloaks and bags and
boxes, and spread white cloths upon them. The
king, pale with grief and hunger, came near, but

36

they set their dogs at him. Nevertheless he greeted them, but they all cried out " Kill him, kill him ! A robber, a devil ! Up with your sticks ! beat him ! break his legs and arms ! He is one of the savage robbers of the woods, he is their spy ; he will bring them all upon us for the sake of our gold and silver. If the rest come it will be all over with us. Out upon him ! "

So all the knaves of those chapmen rushed at him with their clubs, and he was so defenceless, —what could he do but run ?

He escaped into the woods, glad to be quit of that company. After long wandering he found a little hermitage, where a hermit once had lived. It was a wild and savage place, far from all the haunts of men ; but there came into the heart of that English king a hope that here at last he might dwell and end his days, if so be there came to him no new tidings from on high.

CHAPTER VIII.

HOW IT FARED WITH THE QUEEN.

NOW must we tell of the queen and how it fared with her when she was carried off in their ship by those rovers.

Loudly she lamented for the little children so untimely weaned, and for her good lord she loved more than any man born of woman. The sea-rovers treated her not ill, beyond that they carried her away : they gave her two hand-maids to wait upon her ; but nothing they could do might assuage her grief.

Well you may believe there was none aboard the ship but hoped to win her for his own ; and indeed they soon fell to fighting for her sake, but what reason was there why one should take her more than another ?

At last the ship came to land, and sailed into the harbour of Sorlinc.* The anchor was let go, but they were still at blows with noise and clamour

---

*Or Surclin, apparently a corruption of some seaboard place in Suther-land. Gliolas, Gleoalis, or Cleoalis, might be " Gilli " something, hopelessly corrupted in the French versions, but representing the name of the Gaelic lord of a place then near to the Norse earldom of Caithness.

and jealousy who should make the bonny dame his prize.

Now at this port there was a castle, and the usage of the castle was that the lord of the castle should take weel of the wares from whatsoever ship came there into harbourage. There was no jewel so precious but he might claim it of right as his due. This lord was named Glioalis : he was neither king nor earl, but a great man and a good warrior, none better, though he might be somewhat stricken in years. When he was aware that a ship had come into port, and heard that all the men on board were at blows about a lady they had carried away, he made short work of their quarrel saying, " Fight no more ; the lady shall be mine, and that will end the strife. I leave ye all your goods and merchandise—for by St. Nicholas I see right well she is of noble birth ! "

So he carried her into his castle, and gave her into the keeping of his wife ; and in a little while the lady of the castle, seeing her so pretty and withal as modest and shame-faced as any maid, and good and humble, took great love for her. The lady was old like her lord, and after a while she died. Then Glioalis was sorry for her, because they had lived so long together : but when she was buried, and after he had mourned her for the full space, he bethought him that he was now left alone—for they had no children— and he sent for the queen to pray her that she would become his wife.

"Lady," said he, "I will give thee myself and all my lands. When I am gone everything I have shall be thine to thyself, for I have no heirs who might dispute it. When once thou art my wedded wife, and when once my folk have sworn to thee as my lady, there is no man who can take the power away from thee. I know not what more I can promise, but pray thee take me as thy friend and husband."

The lady curtsied low even to the ground. She remembered that she was truly a queen, but that she might not tell her secret. Yet had she rather men burned her or flayed her alive than that she were wedded to another. Neither by force nor prayers, neither for land nor gear, could she take a husband if it were not he who was already her own. She could not believe she might ever see him again, and yet she bethought how she might save herself from sin and shame.

"Fair lord," she answered, "I pray you hear me quietly for a while ; and may God answer your prayers and give you reward for all the kindness I have found in this house of yours. Fair sir, it is not right that you should make a lady out of one who is of vile birth and thrall-born. You are lord of a castle, but my father was a thrall, and I am a poor, silly, wicked woman who have done nothing but folly my life long. My story is all sin and shame ; but, if you will, you shall hear it. Sir, I was a nun. I ran away from my convent ; I lived a wicked, wandering life, among gangrel churls and rascals. Sir, for God's sake, be not angry with me for telling you my tale ; but indeed I am not worthy to loose the shoes from off your feet."

But mark you this, that he had set his heart upon her. He answered, " My dear, all this is not worth two straws ! I care nothing what thou mayest have done or been. All I care for is what thou art and what thou wilt be ! I love thee for thy beauty and thy wit well enough to marry thee ; and as for sins, I have plenty of my own to think upon—follies and faults I have done wilfully. As for low birth, knowest thou not how the chestnut comes sweet and pleasant out of a hard rough husk ? I know not who thy father was ; but if he had been king or emperor thou couldest not be worth more to me. After all, when can you tell what like were folk's fathers ? Many a rascal is of good birth, and many a noble soul of mean breeding. My sweetheart, thus it stands—if thou wilt be mine, I am heartily thine, and let that be an end of the matter. I love thee none the less for the confession ; it is honourable to repent of sin and folly, and shame to shirk the penance of it, and the overcoming. My belief is, thou hast repented and overcome. God has lifted thee up ; it is His will that thou be my wife."

The tears ran out of her eyes and rained over her face ; she could not think what to say. But however he might tempt her she could not bear to give herself away to this man as his wife. Fine it might be to become lady of the land, whatever befell, and to hold the barony at his death ; but then she would rather be burned or drawn asunder by wild horses than prove false to her own wedded lord and husband.

So, being carried this way and that, she bethought her that if she could get respite for a
year, she would keep him off as long as she might,
and within the year find a way out of the coil.
Perhaps even so he might make her a home in his
land, for he seemed willing to believe everything
and do anything.

"Fair sir, for this I pray you grant me a
year's respite. Know that it has been laid upon
me to pass three years in penance, before I should
have pardon for my misdeeds. It was a saint
laid this on me, and if you loved me ten times as
much, still I could not yet be your wife. Two
years have passed, and the third is now at hand.
When this year is over there will have been
waiting enough. Nevertheless, if things were
according to my own desire—if God had not laid
this upon me, and if my soul were not over-
burdened,—you could have wedded me forthwith.
But nay! I am a silly fool to believe such a
thing! You are making a mock of me, I see it
now. It is all a mockery? Tell me, hide it
not! Never talk to me of love in lightness, for
it is cruel to betray a poor silly woman with idle
talk."

"Ah ! " said he, " fair my sweetheart, for God's sake be not so humble and abashed, nor dream that anything I have said is in jest. This matter is so earnest, that it is easy to know whether I have deceived thee in the least little point ! "

" Sir, give me then the boon of respite I have asked, for otherwise it cannot be."

" I grant it," answered he ; " but be sure that I have no will to delay the wedding."

She made answer, for she was very wise, " Fair sir, be it so, since it is your will. But let it not grieve you that I seek the respite."

So he made a proclamation throughout all his country that he would take a truefast and wedded wife, and his will was that she be honoured of all, and that all should serve her and swear to her. Moreover there was none of noble birth or knightly standing but was summoned to the wedding feast.

A crowd of folk came together to the court —knight, vassal, minstrel, falconer and forester, monk regular and canon secular. Before them all he led forth Gratiana to the wedding : and of all the crowd none beheld her but said, " She is

44

no fool, but my lord is in his dotage ! It is his
land she is taking, not himself ; and he, why
he is taking her for herself alone, all because
she has a round white throat and a fair face and
a fresh colour so that my lord's heart is set afire.
She has hooked him and landed him ! Cleverly
she has fished with those eyes of hers, but woe
for my lord's hawking ! Whose counsel did he
seek when he wedded this woman ? Right gay
she will turn, high and mighty, this girl that
cannot be twenty-six as yet ! She will sweep up
all his goods and gear into her apron, and my
lord will have nothing to call his own. Nay, he
will not be worth a dead dog, I warrant it. Well,
it is his own affair ; he may do as he will ; but
I doubt, old as he is, if he sees another year
out ! "

Such like was the talk that passed. When
the tables were drawn he received his wife from
the hands of an abbot, but folk laughed and
jeered among themselves, for the whole thing
was thought a jest. And yet there was game and
glee at the wedding ; there was drinking and
dancing the livelong night ; but little did folk
know that bride and bridegroom were wedded

45

only in name, and spent the dark hours—one in bitter weeping and one in bitter thought.

Next day, before they went their ways, he made them all take their oaths to the lady ; and so they did, seeing that it was his will. Every man did homage to her ; they swore that they would be loyal to her their lives long, and, if it pleased her, they would love her well.

She was well worth their love. So wisely and so sweetly she carried herself that they could not help loving her. Her gentleness and courtesy won them all, so that each man vowed he would be only too glad to please her, and only hoped the time would come when he might show her service and honour.

Well, so it came to pass that before the year was out their lord Glioalis fell ill of a sickness and died. The good queen remained lady of the land, and great and small of their own free will swore their oaths to her anew.

CHAPTER IX.

HOW THE ENGLISH KING BECAME SERVANT TO A CHAPMAN.

WE left the good king in his hermitage where at last he found peace, after suffering pain and sorrow beyond all telling. That hermitage was his abiding place for many a long day, until one night he dreamed a dream, and a vision came to him from the Lord of Heaven, bidding him· depart and leave this quiet sanctuary.

The king prayed God for guidance, and having prayed he took his way through the forest and out of the woods till he came to the seacoast. There he found a company of worthy folk who were at that time setting sail, to voyage overseas into far lands. He went and would join himself to them, but they were not a little taken aback at the sight of him—so lean he was and drawn with hunger that he seemed more like one dead than a living wight. Nevertheless he approached them humbly and falling at their feet besought them, "Lords, for the sake of Jesus, let me come aboard of your ship."

47

Now these chapmen were believers in the true God, and they listened to the prayer.

"Good friend," said one of them, "whence come you? You have suffered greatly; it is plain to see you have fallen among thieves. See, I give you this coat; put it on and cover your nakedness."

The king thanked him for the gift, and put on the coat, and so got him aboard the ship. They sailed out of harbour and away over the high seas, and came safely to haven in the country of Galloway.*

He never thought to reach a land so strange. All abashed and discomfited he stayed on board the ship while others were busy with their going ashore; and for a while it came into his mind that now at last he might tell who he was, and perhaps win friends and living. But then he thought on the command that bade him keep his

---

*"Galinde" or "Gavaide." The other version has it "Spain," but from the lie of the land in the story the place might have been Galloway, where at the period of the supposed action there was a great colony of sea-faring people, part Norse and part Celtic, the Gallgaedhel. "Galinde" may be the copyist's error for "Galuide," (the mistake is easily made in black letter) and Galuide and Galuaide are French forms of "Gallovidia" or "Gallweithia," the Latinized name of Galloway.

secret four and twenty years, and he held his tongue. And yet, being in a strange land and among strangers, the remembrance came afresh to him of his queen and those little children ; and he wept many a tear.

A good man of the country espied him and looked long upon his face ; then coming up he fell gently into talk, saying " Good friend, what is thy name ? "

Thinking of the command which the Voice had laid upon him, the king bowed his head and bethought himself how he might speak truth and yet keep faith. Then said he, " My name is Will."*

The goodman, who was of worthy estate in that land, made answer, " Will, my friend, I cannot but pity thee, for I have seen thy tears. Now tell me what thou canst do, for I should be glad to take thee into my service and give thee a good home. Canst thou draw water from the well ? Canst thou skin eels and feed hens ? Canst thou keep a house in order and groom horses in the stable ? If thou knowest all this to do it well, and if thou wilt be my servant, the

---

*In the French version, "Gui"—for "Guillaume."

wage I bid thee take will be honestly earned."

" Sir," said he, " I will gladly do all this and more. Indeed I may boast that I am no bad groom of horses. You will not find me slothful in your service."

So the rich man took the poor king into his house, and never chapman had so fine a servant. He worked right willingly and never said nay to his master's bidding. There was no sullenness and no malice in his mood ; he never stuck at any service, however irksome or mean. And as it is written, " He that humbleth himself shall be exalted," so it fell out. In course of time he became steward of the house ; never bread or wine or oil was served out but as Will willed. The chapman gave him keys of ark and bower, and trusted him with all his goods. And yet in this betterment of his estate, and amidst all his busy day's work, he often thought of those he had lost, and still at whiles the weeping took him for their sake. But there we must leave him and begin to tell of the two boys and their fortunes.

CHAPTER X.

OF THE TWO CHILDREN AND HOW IT WENT WITH THEM.

YOU have heard that the chapmen who fostered the two boys made sail for Caithness, and being come to port and home again, they christened the lads—one by the name of Wolfling after the wolf which had carried him off and so to say became his godfather, and the other by the name of Seaborn because he was found in a boat upon the sea.

The two foster-fathers were neighbours ; he who had taken Wolfling was called Gonselin, and the other was Foukier. They were worthy enough men, but no fit masters for a pair of young princes. Their life was rough, in that northern land, and their whole minds bent on one thing only, to lay penny on penny by trade and usury until they should be what folk of those parts called well-to-do.

Now if nurture could change nature then these lads would have grown up into such carles as their foster-fathers were. But as the saying goes, "Blood will out." The seedling fig grows up to bear figs, and the tiny thistle-down brings forth its crop of thistles. No art of man can change this law of God.

So the lads waxed and grew amid ignorance and sordid havings, and yet in ten years' time there were not two boys in the world so bonny or so well behaved or so merry of heart. Nature and none other taught them, and it seemed that the evil of the world could never take root in their hearts, which were stony ground for all seeds of baseness.

Being neighbours they were always friends, but never knew they were brothers. Each believed that his foster was his father and had no thought of nearer kindred to his little friend, though always happy in his company. Folk used to say, " Eh, but is not this bairn like yon other ? Look at his hair !—if that one has not the very marrow of it—ay, and the same eyes, and the same nose, and the same mouth and chin ! They are as like as two blades of grass, and their voices—if you heard one you could not tell which without seeing him ; and then they are so fond of each other, they are just like brothers. Nay, it passes aught. They are always together, and care for none of the other children. Well, it must be nature makes it so. Proud, too, I warrant ; see how they never go with lass or lad. "Nay," said every neighbour, "call me nithing if either master Gonselin or master Foukier were in the making of yon two. 'Like to like,' the saying is,—they must be kin; and right it is, for both are pretty lads. Twins they look, and twins they must be, and a bonny pair and all."

So neighbours used to gossip about the two lads, and the upshot of it was they wished them right well and always ended with the old song, "They are no more like Foukier and Gonselin than morning sun is like evening shade."

But whatever neighbours said, the chapmen took counsel together to have the lads brought up to some useful trade, for then they would be better able to buy and sell if they had served their time and knew some craft thoroughly. Master Foukier settled with himself that he would bind Seaborn to the skinner's trade ; and so, one morning he stirred the lad out of bed and told him, "Come, bairn, I'm going to make a skinner of thee."

"My faith!" said the youngster, "Never will I meddle with it! I'll never stitch cloak or fur cape—nay, not unless my playfellow learns along with me!"

When his foster-father heard the lad saying a downright nay to his bidding, and thought that it came of a stiff-necked and a proud spirit, he went forth of the house for a stick, and beat him soundly.

"Naughty brat of a foundling!" he cried; "How darest thou stand against my will?" And then he said, "I found thee in a boat, within sight of the forest of Yarmouth, wrapped up in a rag of an old coat. If ye doubt me, I have kept yon old rag, and there it lies!" said he, going to an ark and fetching it out. He flung it into the lad's face, and swore he would never do anything more for him.

The lad took the rag and thrust it into his bosom. He went out of the house, weeping bitterly, for until then he had always thought he had no other father but the chapman. He rushed forth, half wild, and swore in his heart that he would wander away in the wide world until he found out who he was. And so he went forth of the town.

Now that very same day the very same thing happened to his brother Wolfling in the other house. Master Gonselin bade him go learn a trade, and he answered that he would never go unless his playfellow went with him ; and the man beat him and battered him, and ended with letting out the secret of his birth, and throwing the other bit of a swaddling rag into his face, saying scornfully, " See, there is the pretty proof that shows how thou wast donned when I saved thee from the wolf ! "

But Wolfling, with his face all blubbered over with tears, fell upon his knees, crying, " Sir, you have brought me up, —God reward you for it ! — most kindly until now. I pray you be good to me, and say farewell—for I must away—say farewell without anger. Indeed I belong to you and I always shall belong to you ; I have no right to hate you when you beat me for my good. I owe everything to you. You saved my life and made me all I am. No father could do more for his his real son, and I shall always be yours wherever I am. Indeed I owe you more love and thanks than if you were my real father, for I have the less claim on you."

When the chapman heard him own his debt so prettily, he cooled and said kindly, " There, there, hold thy peace, my dear boy ! It is nought but nonsense. I am sorry I told thee such a parcel of lies, seeing how thou hast taken it to heart ; but forgive me, I was hasty. I said it only to try thee. Thou art my true son, and I love thee best of all the world. Nay, thou art no whit the worse for a word or two ; as they say, 'A clout of mud will draw no blood.' Be in peace and bide with me, and learn to addle thy living same as I do : for mark you, a rich man has many friends. They that get nothing, nothing they will get, and when they grow old never a soul will give a care for them. What ! a poor wise man—in these latter days everyone reckons him a fool ; and a rich fool—everyone calls him wise. Well then, I bid thee and I lay it upon thee—get gear and gold, never mind how. If thou wouldst be thought a wise man, get thee wealth ! "

All this worldly wisdom was utterly thrown away upon the lad. His very nature rose up against his foster-father's trade of usury, and he never could take to such a craft.

"Sir," answered he, "whether all this be right or whether it be wrong, you ought to have no farther charge with me. I have no mind to live upon you unless I am doing your will. You may take this for the last word, that I must have my leave and go my way now, or flit, one day, without leave taken. Loath I should be to run off some fine morning with no farewell; and yet this will be the end of the matter, unless you give me your blessing and let me depart."

"Then, my dear lad, bide the night, and fare the morn."

"Nay, never stay me; it is far to go when once I set forth."

"But thou art not fitted out as I should wish for a long journey."

"That is naught; I want nothing."

"Ay, but thou dost. Thou shouldst have riding-boots of cowhide, and spurs, and a cape against the rain, and then a nag or two. Nay, it will be no great loss to me."

"Ah, sir, God repay you, and give me the chance of rendering these gifts before I die!"

So the chapman gave him a rough woollen cape, which pleased the lad right well, and riding boots and a pair of old spurs. He let bridle and saddle two shod nags, big and swift and good goers ; and he gave him a lad (the French book names him Rodain) for his page. There was nothing in all this to hurt Wolfling's pride, and indeed he was glad and thankful. He had bow and arrows of his own, and made the lad carry them. Then master Gonselin lent him money to the value of one mark, and gave him this parting word, —" Never lend without sureties, no matter who it be. That is my last will and warning."

(But master Gonselin for once was better than his word).

Now Wolfling was bound for his adventure. He bade farewell and turned away : but one thing grieved him, that he could not find his playfellow to say good-bye to him. He supposed he would be somewhere about the town, and so thought Seaborn of Wolfling. They were both setting forth into the world, heavy-hearted and alone, neither knowing that the other was in the very same plight.

CHAPTER XI.

HOW THE TWO BOYS FOREGATHERED IN THE FOREST OF CAITHNESS.

WOLFLING rode away on horseback for a while, over the fell; and at last, coming down a brow, he saw somebody before him yonder in the dale. Of course he could not guess who it was, for he had no thought of finding his playfellow there; but he spurred his nag and rode at a gallop down the hill to overtake the wayfarer.

The other was aware of two folk galloping after him, and wondered who in the world they might be. At first he thought they were robbers, and then that perhaps they were come to catch him and bring him back to the town. So the best he could do was to run, and make as fast as he could for the woods; he was lithe and slender, and he might hide in a bush and never be found again. And so it happened that Seaborn, like a fool, was running away from his best friend and rushing on his worst fate, for it was no laughing matter to be lost in that forest. He ran for his life, as though the king's officers were behind him : but Wolfling on horseback soon caught him up.

Mightily ashamed and abashed he felt when he saw who it was, for he made no doubt that Wolfling had heard all about the quarrel, and was come to scold him and bring him home again. But Wolfling was full of joy when he found it was his playmate. He flung from his horse and kissed him, saying,—" Mate of mine, I was a woeful lad, starting away without thee. I thought thou wast somewhere with thy father. Tell me, dear friend, has thy father quarrelled with thee too ? "

At that, Seaborn lifted up his eyes—for he had held them downcast for very shame, and now he guessed that Wolfling knew nothing. He hardly dared to say all, for he thought it too utterly terrible and disgraceful ; and only said that he had been beaten and turned away from the house with dreadful threats, for they wanted to make him a skinner ! " A skinner ! Only think of it ! Away with their beastly pelts ! " he cried.

" Dear lad, but that is the very thing, my word upon it, that my father wanted to do with me. He wanted to make me—I don't know what—a stinking wild-cat or a mart. And then because I dared say no, he beat me, and it hurt! For all that, I have my heart's desire. See, I am out and away on my travels with clothes and gear; and if only thou wilt go with me—I can take thee up on horseback—there is nothing thou shouldst lack. Indeed I would not mind my father's anger so much if thou went with me. We could shape our course together and help one another as hand helps hand."

"Nay, I cannot see ahead; I cannot think where luck may lead us."

"Well, we have money enough for this little while, and before it is spent we may light upon some lord who will take us into his service. We can hardly fail of that."

In this talk they went on their way together, building up hopes and plans as lads do; and yet neither of them dared say a word of those two bits of swaddling-clothes which each kept safe in his bosom and trusted to help him in the one thing his mind was set upon—to unravel the secret of his birth.

Their road lay inland through the forest, and as they went they spied a young hart, leaping out of a thicket and away.

" Shoot ! " cried Seaborn, " shoot ! "

" That will I," said Wolfling, " never fear."

He took an arrow from his page lad and knocked it on the bow-string. The hart ran no further than an open glade and there browsed, as if waiting for the shot. Wolfling aimed true, and it fell dead without a struggle, while Seaborn clapped his hands in glee at his friend's good marksmanship. They ran toward their quarry, and threw it across one of the horses, while the page rode behind on the other.

At last they came to a clear spring where the water ran fresh and clean over fine gravel that shone like silver. All round it the trees were stately and tall and the grass was thick and green, and close at hand was a little lodge, newly built, it seemed. They alighted from their horses and went in.

The first thing they saw was a collar of gold hanging from a beam in the house. They looked and searched all round, but nothing else whatever they found ; and yet the little cabin was fairly built of boughs from the trees, watertight and well thatched above, without other signs of any who might dwell in it.

They were glad to find such a harbour for the night, and Wolfling said—" My counsel is that we take up our abode here. Rodain knows this part of the country-side ; he can go out and see if there be any living folk who will sell us bread and fire and salt."

" I will go," said he, " and gladly. Farther along this path there is a house of monks, and they will help us. I think they will give me bread and salt, ay, and a little wine too."

So away he went, and the two lads busied themselves in skinning and cutting up the hart ; and when their venison steaks were ready for cooking, one of them went out to look for the page.

He did not keep them waiting long. He said he had not far to seek before he found the monks' door, and when he asked for what they needed he got it easily. The abbey cellar was so big, he said, that he had never seen anything like it. He had forgotten nothing of his errand, and brought a lap-full of bread and salt, and fire to cook the venison, and as much wine as they could drink.

They were not too proud to unload him, and

to carry the wine, bread, salt and fire into the lodge. All three turned kitchen-knaves, and as they roasted their venison upon the spit they said to one another how jolly it was to be living in the forest, and how they would like to stay there for ever so long, if they were not in such a hurry to go forward and seek their fortunes!

CHAPTER XII.

HOW THE BOYS WERE BEFRIENDED BY THE EARL OF CAITHNESS.

NOW just as their meat was ready cooked, and they were going to make their feast, who should come in but the forester !

You must know that these woods belonged to the earl of Caithness,* the lord of all this country ; and no one might hunt or shoot there be he never so rich and powerful, stranger and neighbour alike, but the earl. It was for that reason the forester was living there, to keep watch and ward upon the woods.

When he found strangers making free in the fine new lodge he had just built for himself, he stood amazed in the doorway. Seaborn greeted him courteously, but they could see that he was fairly struck dumb with astonishment and anger, and gave them not a word in answer to their good-day.

" I have caught you ! " he said at last.

---

*The great Earl of Caithness, in the time to which this story must refer, was Thorfinn Sigurdsson (about 1009-1064) for whose life see the *Orkneyinga-Saga.*

65

"This is a hanging matter. You have come to the wrong port, my lads! By the God in whom I believe, I will take you before the earl, and he will hang you or head you. That is his deer you have taken. The least he will do is to chop off your hands or pluck out your eyes."

"My dear sir," said Wolfling, "God forbid! We have done nothing to hang for, I think. At any rate, let us cry truce for to-night, and to-morrow morning we will go with you wherever you like. See now, we will give you all the money we have, if that will make peace. We have the worth of a mark in silver, and so please you we will give it up. Take it, and deal easily with us, for we have nothing more in the world. If we could, we would make it more, without further ado, but that is all we have."

"Let us see the money first," said the forester. "Time enough to talk when it is in my hand."

The page carried the purse ; so he brought it out and untied the strings. Then he poured all the silver pennies into the forester's hands.

"Well, well," said the churl, "say no more. Let us call it peace then." He made sure of the money with a grin—the greedy rascal—and when he had stowed it safely away, " Now then, lads," he said, " make yourselves easy, and never mind me ! "

So they all sat down together and made a night of it. There was plenty to eat and drink, and they laughed and talked, and when they were sleepy lay down in their cloaks upon the ground, for there was neither straw-bed nor fur-rug to lie upon.

In the morning, as soon as the day began to dawn the forester stirred and woke. Rodain the page went and got their horses and made them ready. Then the forester led the way—he knew the country well—and took them by so straight a road that before the time of evensong they came into the presence of the earl of Caithness.

The lads bowed low and said nothing ; the forester was ready with his speech.

" My lord," said he, " these lads I bring you were wandering through the woods and happened to kill one of your lordship's deer. Of course, my lord, I have brought them up for judgment, and your lordship will deal with them. But if I may be allowed to say so, it would be rough to take the law of such young lads. I would never have brought them up here, upon my soul, only I am your lordship's faithful servant, and bound as such to do my duty. It is my sense of duty, my lord, makes me bring them up before your lordship."

"Enough," said the earl, "It was well done. They seem fine lads, and clever ones. They may stay here at my court. If they behave themselves wisely and seemly, they shall be rewarded as they deserve."

"Fair lord earl," replied Wolfling, "there is nothing in the world we should like better. Many thanks to you. We are greatly beholden for this favour."

"Lad," said the earl, "you are welcome, thou and thy brother—for brothers you be, I doubt not ? "

"My lord," replied Wolfling, "it is not for me to say nay to you. But we are neither brothers nor any sort of kinsmen. He will bear me witness, too."

"Peace ! " cried the earl. "This is folly. No two lads could be so like and not akin. You are brothers, only you dare not say it ; may be there is some mystery. But what matter ? Tell me thy name."

"Lord," he answered, "they call me Wolfling; there's no secret about that; and my mate and dear friend, they call him Seaborn."

The Earl asked no more questions, but bade that the lads be taken care of, under the eye of one of his men, who was to be their master and teacher in all that belonged to hunting and falconry. He used to carry them with him to the woods and to the river, and that was the way he taught them the art and craft of hawk and hound.

Before long the earl took notice of them that they were bold and clever beyond other lads, and he loved them for it, and gave them gifts, whatever their mind was set upon. He let them have fine horses and rich clothes to their hearts' content. He liked them to follow him in the woods whenever he was shooting or hunting, and they for their part had no wish to leave him. So they became great hunters, chasing the hart and the doe and all manner of wild beasts of the forest; and it seemed they had a kind of natural talent and love for hounds and hawks, for though they had not been brought up to such crafts they very soon learnt all they needed to know. Everyone, great and small, thought well of them; and when they were twenty years old they were strong of limb and supple of body, so that they beat all comers at feats of arms, and the earl, for the love he bore them, made them his knights.

Now this strange thing came about that the earl of Caithness, who was so fond of these two lads, was all the while a bitter enemy of their mother ; for the lands of Sorlinc where the widow of Glioalis, once queen of England, bore rule, marched with Caithness ; and for the sake of joining these lands to his, the earl had offered her marriage. But as you may well guess, she would not ; so he made war upon her, to bend her and her folk to his will. This war still went on, and of all the knights of Caithness none were so keen and none wrought so much havoc in the lands of Sorlinc as these two youngsters. For the love and duty they bore the earl they hated and harmed the lady all they might ; and often they said if they could only make her their prisoner they would gladly burn her alive !

But of this hereafter.

CHAPTER XIII.

HOW THE KING CAME BACK TO ENGLAND.

ALL this long while king William had been servant to that chapman in the land of Galloway; and so faithful was he found that his master gave everything into his hand, to rule his house and hold his havings entirely, never even asking him for the reckoning of what he spent or served out. He was fully trusted, because he was known to be trustworthy.

One fine day the chapman took counsel and said—"Will, if thou wilt, I will lend thee four pounds of silver of my moneys and thou mayest go on thine own errands to England or Flanders or France, and make thine own bargains. If thou canst buy and sell at the great fairs over seas there is no fear but thou wilt grow rich. I ask no share of what thou mayest make, but only to have my own again; the profit is for thee. Sad it is to see good folk brought low by poverty and loss of their substance, and thou hast been brought very low. I would see thee set up again, and if thy gains by this voyage are two hundred marks, not a penny will I touch."

The king gave him great thanks. " But I should like to bring you back all the money I make. Since this is your rede, I am bound to follow it. I will not miss a market or a fair, where I am likely to do good business. I see my way to deal in leather and alum and many other goods to great profit."

So the chapman gave him the money and the king was not long in making himself ready to go on his cheaping errand. He laid out his money on all sorts of ventures, some easy and safe, and some dark and risky ; but never missed a chance at fair or market ; and before a great while was past he had taken far more than his master had lent him, for he was lucky and fortunate beyond all the other chapmen.

When he came home again, bringing more than had ever been known to be gained in one voyage, his master was full of wonder, and held him dearer than before. He knew that Will was a good steward, but now he found him a lucky and canny merchant. He was never tired of telling folk what a treasure he had found, and

72

nothing would suit him but to send his two sons
on a voyage with Will, to be under him and learn
the craft of cheaping. He would let him have a
ship, and wares worth a thousand marks—nay,
he would make it three thousand ; they should
go to the famous markets away yonder in France
—nay, first he would have him try England ;
there would be a great fair at Bristol next week,
that should be their first errand. Will should
have his own ship, and his two sons ; strictly he
bade them look to Will, and never be so bold as
to say him nay in anything. He would trust him
with them,—" And mind you, lads, whatever he
says to you, do it."

Well, they weighed anchor, the king and the
chapman's two sons in his charge, for Bristol, in a
ship loaded with rich wares. It was fine weather,
and the wind was fair, the sea nowise rough or
stormy, and they set sail with great gladness and
good hope. They had a skipper who understood
his craft of steering a ship, and knew all that a
seaman knows of the look of the sea and the lead of
the stars. The sails carried them merrily through
the waves, and the round ship ploughed her way
over the sea, so that they made no long voyage of it.

At the haven for Bristol they unloaded their goods, and all the horses they had on board, for that was great part of their cargo, fine nags, easy going, swift and strong for the English market. They worked hard at this job of unloading, and yet it took them all day to get through it ; so great a mass of wares they had brought. Next day they went up to the town.

At this time the land was ruled by a young man, who was king William's own nephew. Folk had made him king, rather than any other, because he was the next heir to the crown. So this young king had come to Bristol the day before with a great following to see the fair. But the town was big, and our king William was in another quarter of it, busy in setting up his booth and laying out his goods.

We need not say that he was no less lucky than before. He sold his wares freely, and got good prices from all who bargained with him. There was no cheating him, for he knew what his things were worth ; he asked the right price, and got it.

Now while he was at his booth, overseeing the sale of his goods, he espied a young man

74

wearing an ivory horn, and called him in. The young man came in at the first word, and king William asked what he would take for the horn he carried. When the young man rightly understood what the stranger asked—" It is well worth a gold piece," said he.

" Then sell it to me," said the king.

" Right willingly, for my price," answered he.

" What price is that ? "

" No less than five silver shillings."

" Five shillings ? "

" Not a farthing less."

" Thou shalt have them, if thou wilt tell me where thou didst find that horn."

" As I am asked, sir, I will tell how I got it. A long while ago, when king William, my lord —and a great and good man he was,—went out of sight along with his wife—and a good lady all men held her to be—and never a soul knows now what became of them—well, when they were lost, the servants in their household 'swept the house' as the saying is: they ransacked hall and bower, and made away with everything they could find. I was a little lad then, and I had always been brought up in the king's house.

Nobody warned me, and so I went hunting with the rest of them—ay, and the best of them, for high and low of the king's meinie joined in that game, as the old custom was. We scoured the place, and turned everything upside down ; and for my part I found the horn ; under a bench it was, and I crept in and laid hand on it. Whether I was right or wrong never came into my head, but I have always kept it since that day. Now it is laid upon me to go on a pilgrimage, and if I sell this horn it would only be that I may have somewhat to bestow in alms upon the poor. I have no mind to make anything for myself out of my old master's goods."

"Well said!" answered the king : and added that it might still be something to the young man's good, if he did as he meant. As he had no money in his hand, he bade one of his men pay over the five shillings, and of course he did so—grumbling the while at this bad business, for the old horn seemed mighty dear at the value of a good ox or more. The young man went through the market scattering his money right and left to the poor, so that his pilgrimage was soon begun.

CHAPTER XIV.

HOW KING WILLIAM TALKED WITH THE NEW KING WHO REIGNED IN HIS STEAD.

NOW there were many people at the Bristol fair who had known king William in the days of his reign, and as they passed by his booth could not but see how like this stranger was to their ancient lord. Many stood still to stare at him, and all day long there were knots of folk lingering and looking less at the wares than the chapman. By and bye some of them went to the young king and told him there was one in the town so very like king William they could hardly know whether it were not he, come again in the flesh.

"What is his name?" asked the young king. "Have you found out who he is, and whence he comes?"

"No, my lord; nobody knows him, and we have not liked to ask."

"Go then," said he, "and get into talk with this chapman. If he is at all like my uncle he will not be hard to come at, and we shall get on well together. Beg him come to me. Say I would have him at my court. I should like to keep him near me ; he would remind me of my uncle every time I looked at him. Nay, I must go and find him myself ; I am eager to see this man."

So the young king set off, riding a great Spanish horse, and a fair throng of his men followed at his back ; for his mind was full of the thought of seeing once more a face like one he loved. Of course nobody could tell for certain that the stranger was really king William, who had been as good as dead these twenty-three years ; and nobody dared say it might be he, though if they had only known it, how glad they would have been !

The young king never drew rein, but pricked on ahead of the throng that followed him, until he came to the booth. He flung from his horse and fell upon the chapman's neck and kissed him saying, " Fair sir, I come to ask you if you are king William. Tell me, for love's sake ! Folk are all saying, fair sir, how like you are to him. For God's sake, dear sir, tell us. If we knew it, and if thou wert really my uncle, these lords and I myself would be your men and serve you this very hour."

King William knew his nephew at once, and when he heard these words he could not think what answer to make. " My lord," he said at last, " for God's sake, let be ! I am not here to be mocked and made a fool of, but to sell the wares I have brought like an honest chapman."

" Well, friend," said the young king, " I am fain to see thy face. Sit down by me and let us talk together for a while."

" As ye please," answered king William. " But I may not sit beside you ; my place is here on the ground at your feet, for by all seeming ye are far too high a man for the likes of me."

" Nay, never fear. I am the king, and thou —why, thou art as like an uncle of mine as the balas stone is like a carbuncle, or as the blooms of the briar are like roses—which is as much as to say thou art his very image. I loved him, and for his sake I love thee so that it is on my tongue to call thee uncle and lord—ay, I had near said my king ! There never was such a wonder ! It is the strangest adventure ever happened ! Friend, thou hast been long enough selling grain

79

and alum and wax. Come to my court beside the Thames, and thou shalt have everything in my gift to bestow—so God save me, thou shalt ! If it mislike thee not, I will make thee my seneschal."

"Seneschal ! God bless me ! Indeed and truly, my good lord, I have no mind for such an honour. It is so high a climb for me that I should miss my footing and fall ; and a fall like that would break me to pieces with grief. It is no new thing to see men of low degree raised so high that they died of their dignities. Never tempt me to such a bane ! Nay, my lord, bestow that gift on one who can use it, and let the poor chapman stick to his calling. Why, some day it might happen that your king came again, and then what a fall for me to go back to my cheaping and hold a booth at the fairs ! I have no liking for that adventure ! But, my lord, you yourself who are king, tell me—so please you—what would you do if he came again ? "

"I should be glad, indeed I should ! So God save me, I would give him back the crown I am only keeping for him—and for the well-being of the land. I would never think twice about it, for I hold myself no more than his reeve, ruling in his name until he come. It is for his sake I wish it—and pray thee to be my friend. Come and bide with me as friend with friend ; thou shalt eat in my hall every day and bring what folk with thee thou wilt ; there shall be fire and fodder for all ; and then when thou goest thy way all thou hast lost I will make up to thee from the tolls and dues the other chapmen pay, so that thy time will not be wasted. Say ' ay ' to this — it is a fair offer : and meantime take it not ill if I ask thy name and home, for I ask it in all courtesy and nowise to thy hurt."

" King, they call me Will and I come from the land of Galloway. Yonder are the wares I sell, and I reckon to carry back a good shipload of cloth and English wool."

So they talked and in a while the young king took his way with many an offer, frankly and freely made, of good service. Indeed he served his new friend far beyond his word, and as long as they were together in the town he never wearied of showing him kindness and courtesy. All the folk of the place dealt in such a way that king William could easily believe he kept the heart of

England. If ever God brought him back to his estate, there would be no murmurings, no treasons, no stand against his rule : —that was plain. But while he was at Bristol he kept himself close, and was careful never to betray his secret ; and when at last his time was spent, he slipped away taking no leave of his nephew, the young king.

CHAPTER XV.

HOW THE KING CAME TO SORLINC.

ONE morning, then, king William the chapman slipped out of the town of Bristol at daybreak and rode down to the seashore where his ship was lying. He had already got all his wares aboard, what he had bought and what he had taken in cheaping for the goods he bartered, and no richer shipload would you find betwixt this and the great mart of Aleppo. The skipper, Terfes was his name, had made the ship ready, and they were soon out of port and away on the high sea.

But in a while the breeze freshened and the sea rose ; a storm came on. " Yare ! yare ! " cried the mariners as they shortened sail in haste, but all to no purpose. The waves broke so violently that the ship was thrown off her course, and driven down the coast upon a lee shore. So near the cliffs they scudded that it seemed they would break their yards against the rocks : and when they were past that danger they were in a wild water, with waves running mountain-high and valley-deep, where they could get no way on, but tossed and plunged and drifted, they knew not whither. Darker and darker grew the sky, and more terrible the gale. Now and again they tried to get her head round, but there was no standing against the storm. Even the skipper lost heart amid this battle of the elements, when the thunder roared and the lightning flashed, and all the four winds of heaven were let loose to war upon the deep. What could he do but give the ship her head and let her drive ? And then it was like folk at the ball-play,—one wave cast her at another ; up to the clouds she was hurled, and down she fell into the depths. The sail was in ribbons and the mast in splinters. Every soul aboard gave himself up for lost. Loud they called on God and the Holy Cross : —" Help, good St. Nicholas, help ! We commend us to God's mercy. Oh ! pity us, good Lord, and assuage these winds ; atone their strife, for wherefore do they strive ? In this their warring we are the slain. Oh ! great and terrible is their might, these princes of the power of the air ! Like the lords of earth they go forth to war, and who shall know the cause ? Like the lords of the earth who for their pleasure burn down the habitations of men, and overthrow fenced castles, even so are these ; and we are they who be slain in the madness of their warfaring ! " So cried they all upon the good Lord, as they reeled to and fro, and staggered like drunken men on the deck of their ship.

For a space of three days the storm continued so fell and foul that they never knew where they might be, nor ever ate morsel nor drank drop. On the fourth day at dawn there was a rift in the clouds, and it brightened as the day broke. The sea was quieter, and settling down little by little ; and the winds made peace one with another, it seemed, for there was but one gentle breeze blowing steadily and softly, a good wind that swept the clouds away and cleared the air.

Now at last the skipper could take his bearings and make some guess at the shore to which they were coming,—for it so happened that they were not far away from land.

" Ship-master," said the king, " where are we ? Knowest thou yonder town ? "

" Ay, sir, that I do. I know it too well.

Nay, I will tell ye no lies, but if you make this haven it will cost you dear. Yonder is the spot where a chapman falls among thieves, and one thief is the lord and another is the lady of the land. There is nought so fine among his wares, there is none of his lading so costly, but the lord of that castle may take it, of old use and wont, ay, and ransack the ship to come at it. And then, when he has done, the lady takes her turn, and sweeps up after him, until there's nothing left worth keeping."

Well, said the king, there was no choice left but to make yonder harbour, for to land they must get, and that without waste of time. Hard work it was, but the mariners made shift with broken oars and bits of spars to bring the ship into port, safe at last, though with much ado.

In the fields before the castle the folk of the place were holding sports ; but no matter ; as soon as they set eyes on the ship they sent a man down to ask whether she were long-ship or trading-buss. He ran down to the staithe and hailed the newcomers—what was their errand and what country-folk ? It was the king himself who gave answer, " We are chapmen from Galloway."

The messenger said no more, but ran back to the castle crying,—" Up ! haste ! Chapmen come to the port ! "

Never a soul thought twice on it, but away to the staithe. There went aboard first the lady of the land to claim weel of the wares, and next after her the seneschal, who had his port dues to take, and so forth.

Now when the lady came nigh the ship the chapman-king stepped forward at once to meet her ; but sore he took it that he could not catch sight of her face, by reason that the lady had drawn up her wimple over it. Nevertheless, he greeted her courteously, saying, " Fair lady, welcome aboard ! I know your errand, for I am not unaware of the custom of this harbourage. And now we have a richer ship-load than ever trading-buss carried. Of the wares under my hand ye shall have your heart's desire, if that is in my power."

" Friend, it must needs be that I turn over the wares one by one : and when I have seen everything, then, if eyes of mine can tell it, the best will I take ! "

So she came aboard, and her heart beat hard

in her breast, for it began telling her already of one she knew of old, though as yet she could not be sure that this was indeed the king.

All the costliest and best in his lading he had out for to show her—wefts fit for an emperor, orphreys for a pope's robe, coverlets of price, furs of sable and ermine, tables of silver and ouches of gold. But yonder hung an old horn from the broken mast of the ship, and it caught her eye as she looked from this to that. What were all these brave and bonny things beside it? And she looked again and again, but it would not wholly come to mind. At the chapman, busied in unpacking his wares, she looked, and then at the horn, and then at him; and oh! what a pain took her at the heart. There was nothing for it, but when his back was turned, she must cast away all shame, and take the horn in her hand, and kiss it, and when she kissed it her pain was somewhat eased. She looked at it long and fondly, saying no word to any, and turned to meet the chapman.

Fair seemed the day to her, and a glad and happy woman was she. Down beside him on the deck she sat, and on his hand she spied her ring.

Well, when she saw the ring she knew it at once, and " Fair sir," she said, " of all your wares my eyes have seen there is nothing will content me but yonder ring. Give me that, and you shall be quit."

" Ah, lady," said he, " say not so ! That were no easy quittance for me ! In this ship there is lading so wealthy that a hundred marks of gold would not buy it. Take all if you will, but leave me my ring. Why, between the gold and the jewel it is not worth a single ounce of money ; and yet I hold it dear. By the faith I owe, my whole life is on my finger, so long as I wear that ring. Take it away and ye slay me ! "

" Come, come, sir chapman ; fair and softly ! Ye can easily buy such another. If this is my choice, how will you withstand me ? It is not for me to go on my knees to thee ! What ? wilt thou play the fool and say me nay, when I ask such a trifle ? This morsel of gold is a mere nothing to that which my rights give me. What is there of thine I may not take, if it were thy uttermost farthing ? "

" Lady, I cannot think why ye may not be otherwise contented. Must it be so ? Then

I have no choice but to give way. But ye know not how great the gift is, nor how unwillingly given. It is out of my very heart ye have plucked it, if it must never come again upon my finger. It is my very life I have rendered up. God give you and me joy of the bargain!"

Fain she was of those words! And yet she dissembled still, and thanked him courteously enough, taking the ring and putting it on her finger. "Friend," she said, "for guerdon of this ring you shall have no guesting but mine. You and all your fellows shall be lodged with me to-night. Here in my town ye shall find a market for all your goods; this I desire and entreat."

Sore her people wondered, and great folly they thought it, that she took no more than a ring when she could have a hundred marks' worth if she were but wiser. You may be sure the seneschal never spared of his chance. He left not an apple's worth of his tolls and dues, customs and harbour rights; and took them in the best wares he could find.

So then she went back to her castle, taking with her the king as an honoured guest, and his whole company bidden to dine with her : and yet all this while he could not see her face, though his heart burned within him for a glance at it.

She bade set the tables, and that was done speedily : there was no lack of servants in her hall : and then they brought water to wash her hands—so pretty and white they were. The king came near to hold her sleeves ; but she said laughing, " This rich chapman is too wealthy to serve so poor a lady. Nothing of mine is worth the semblance you have made of service. Now, sir chapman, it is thy turn to wash. Be at ease ; give thy commands as if thou wert come to the place of thy heart's content."

When they had washed they went to table. She made them bring her guest to the high-seat, side by side with herself, and they ate together. Then at last she must withdraw the wimple that hid her face, and brought it down to her chin. Red she blushed when she let herself be seen. He looked at her and she looked him in the face, and he knew for a truth that it was she.

Ay, she knew it too : but neither of them dared ask, " Art thou still mine ? "

CHAPTER XVI.

HOW KING WILLIAM HUNTED THE STAG OF SIXTEEN TINES.

FOR a while they talked of this and that, these two who were man and wife but dared not avow it, sitting side by side at the feast in the hall of Sorlinc. When dinner was nearly over, the hounds were brought in, and the sight of those hounds put him that was once a king in mind of the days when he went hunting : for in old times there was nothing he loved more than the woods and the chase, riding to hounds and following the deer in the forest. It all came back to him like a dream.

Never think (says our French book) that we are putting an idle tale upon you ; for people can dream without falling asleep. There are wandering thoughts as misleading as any visions of the night. You need never doubt our story if it tells you nothing more unbelievable than this of the king's waking dream.

Well ; he sat there silent and musing until he fancied he was beside a river in a forest,

chasing a stag of sixteen tines ; there it was
fleeing before him ; the hunt after it hot-foot,
and he, as of old, halloaing to his hounds. Everything else slipped out of mind. " Hey, lads !
Hark forward ! He is off ! "

The whole hall burst out laughing. He had
been thinking aloud, and never a soul in the
place but heard him shout. " Yonder chapman
is out of his wits ! " they said one to another,
" See how foolish he looks ! "

But the lady understood. She drew him
gently towards her, and he started, as one who is
waked suddenly out of sleep. Very sweetly she
spoke—" My lord, my friend "—as one who
loved him dearly,—and put her two arms about
his neck, begging him to tell why he had
shouted so.

" Lady,—I remember it all. Must I tell
thee ? I will try. I was thinking—believe me,
I was thinking—I thought myself hunting the
greatest stag I ever beheld. I could not catch it,
but the dogs were so close I thought they were
upon it. Was I asleep and dreaming ? Upon
my word I never knew ! "

She was far too wise to laugh at him, for

well she remembered how he loved hunting. So she just kissed him.

Folk in the hall thought she too had lost her wits, but little they knew about it. She was thinking of nothing in the world but to give him pleasure.

" Would it please you, my dear lord," she said, " to go to the woods this very afternoon ? Should you thank me if I came too ? "

" Should I thank you ? " he cried. " Ay, that I would, heartily. There is nothing I love so dearly ; but ah, lady ! these four and twenty years I have had sorrow enough and to spare."

" Sir, by St. Paul I swear it, and these arms that hold you, if I can ensure it, you shall see your dream come true."

So the lady bade her hunters don their attire, couple the hounds and saddle the horses. They bestirred themselves and there was no long delay before each was arrayed according to his need, and none was left wanting horn and harness. Away they rode into the woods, and there, in a lone spot, they found that very stag with the sixteen tines, and laid the hounds at him.

Forward went the stag with leaps and bounds,

94

and they after him shouting. The hunt was up, the hounds gave tongue, and followed him through the forest that resounded to their baying. And as they rode side by side, they fell into talk, the king and the lady—for who was there could overhear them ? And as they talked, happy tears they shed,—and who was there to mark ? But if any of that gay company had known the tale that came piecemeal forth, the long years of wandering and waiting, hard must his heart have been to withstand the pity of it, and the joy of that foregathering.

Little by little she told him her story—how Glioalis had taken her to wife ; under what covenant ; how he died within the year ; how the lordship of land and port came into her keeping without let or hindrance from any : and then she went on with the tale.

"There is an earl," she said, "whose borders march with mine. Fain is he to have me wedded, and many a time he has asked me. For the nay I give him, he makes everlasting war upon me ; even now this war is afoot, in all its bitterness and fierceness. Why do I name it now but to warn you ? This wood where we

95

ride, it lies between him and me. Dear my lord,
I would counsel you,—I pray you,—beyond all
other thing I bid you beware of the river that
parts this wood of mine from his forest. If the
stag runs yonder, and swims the river, turn back,
I beg and pray you. Never pass that river, for on
the farther side are our bitter foes ! "

He would try to bear it in mind, he said.
If he had not brought the stag to bay before he
came to the river, he would turn back—unless he
forgot.

"On that agreement," said the lady, "I
give you leave to follow the stag. Ride on, dear
lord ; I will not hold you back. I will ride fair
and softly while you finish the chase."

So the king bade her a short farewell, and
galloped toward that side where he heard the
baying of the hounds and the noise of the hunt.
The stag was hard pressed, but still it held its
course ; and one and another fell behind until
the king alone was left with the hounds. They
came to a river ; the stag ran wildly down the
bank and swam for its life. After it went the
hounds, all swimming the broad stream. After
them rode the king and pushed his horse into

deep water, and swam it over—utterly heedless of the warning, nor stopping to think in the heat of the chase, whether this were the dangerous river he had been so strictly forbidden to cross.

On the farther bank the hounds were upon their quarry. By main weight and strength they dragged it to ground, and when he came up to them the great stag of sixteen tines was taken.

CHAPTER XVII.

HOW THE KING FOUND HIS TWO SONS AGAIN.

NOW when King William saw that the stag was taken, he set horn to mouth and blew the Prise. Three times he took breath and sounded, and the note rang far and wide through the woods.

As it happened, there were two knights of the earl of Caithness riding along out yonder, and when they heard that horn, pricked their horses hastily toward the sound of it. They rode all armed with shield and sword, and coats of mail, ready to slay the stranger who was so bold as to hunt their lord's deer, or at the least to take him and bring him bound to the earl's castle.

It was not until he was aware of these two riding towards him that the king brought to mind his trespass, and knew how he had sinned against the charge his love had laid upon him. He saw them come straight over against him, one with sword drawn and the other with shield on arm, threatening and crying out, " Knave, by what reason, by what right, darest thou hunt in this wood ? "

The king had alighted from his horse, and he was all unarmed but for his hunting knife ; so when he heard their words of wrath and scorn he fled to a great oak tree that grew near by, and plucking out his knife, made a shield of the stout tree-bole.

"Ye are a dead man, knave, unless you yield," they cried. "Ye can never stand against us. Die then, or cry our mercy!"

The king, as one who saw death before his eyes, made answer, "Mercy, my lords! Mercy, I pray! But mark you this; if you had slain me it had been the worse for you!"

"What, sir knave? How? A threat and a prayer? None but a fool grants mercy for menace." And to one another they said,— "Fellow of mine, we must not spare him. He threatens us for his death; let him do his worst!"

So they both rushed upon him, and he, in the fear of his life, covered himself as best he might, now behind the oak tree, and now behind his horse.

"Lords," he said at last, "ye will do an ill day's work when you have slain me, unless ye would kill a king."

99

" A king ? " they cried.

" Ay, truly," said he.

" Of what land ? "

" England ! "

" What then are ye doing here ? What adventure is this ? "

They held their hands, and he began to tell them. To hear his tale they alighted from their horses and drew near ; and he made known to them in a few words how he left his realm, and how in so brief a space wife and sons were taken from him ; — his queen reft away by sea-rovers — and each heaved a sigh for the pity of it : his two children lost that very day, — and they could not refrain from tears. But when he went on to tell them how he had cut off the skirts of his robe and lapped the two lads in the rags ; how he carried one down to the sea shore and laid it in a boat ; how, when he thought to find the other it was seized by a wolf, and he chased it until he fell out-wearied, and then coming back to the sea shore found nothing of the other, — why, the weeping laid hold upon each of them, and they sobbed — it was a wonder to see !

Well, he went on with his tale ; and the

next thing was about the purse with the golden byzants which the chapman had thrown him ; and how the eagle had swooped down upon it, and cast him to the ground.

Now befell the most marvellous adventure of all. For just as he had come to this place in the story, a very miracle happened. Out of the clouds, as a gift straight from God in heaven, somewhat dropped at his feet, evenly betwixt them as they stood there talking. It was a purse of gold ! The king stooped and took it in his hand. It was the very purse ; and lo, an eagle, sailing away yonder over the tree-tops !

"Sir," said one of the knights, full of wonder and amazement, "of a surety God hath shown us, in His mercy and goodness, that the tale is true, beyond any doubting ! "

And hastily broke in the other,—"Fair lord, so God love me, I have never known my father. Ye are my father. I am your son. Ay, the good man who fostered me said I had been carried off by a wolf. He told me where and how. In his anger and scorn he gave me the very rag of a robe that happed me when I was a foundling. I have it still. So please you, ye shall know the whole truth of it, whether I am indeed your son or no. Because of that wolf they call me Wolfling. Nay, I need say no more ; the truth is the truth ! "

They gazed at one another, all three, in amazement for a while. Then spoke the third, and said what he had never breathed to any living man.

" God," he said, " has brought me hither. Now I know what I never knew before. All my life I have had my own brother by me, and thought it not. Mate of mine, we two have been long in good fellowship, but now it is clear beyond all manner of doubt we are twins and brothers, — and ye, fair sir, are our father ! In a boat on the seashore, that was where they found me. In a rag of a robe I was lapped ; I found it in my home and kept it carefully up to this day. O fully and plainly will the truth come out ! "

Said the king, " It is the Lord's doing, and it is marvellous in our eyes ! But, my fair knights, those rags of a robe—ye must bring them and show, if ye would have me know past doubting that all this is true."

" Come away, then," cried they. " Ye shall see them. What more do we ask ? "

"So be it," said the king. "And yet, what of our stag? Must we not brittle him first?"

"Well said!" they answered; and it was not before they had made a seemly end to the hunt of the stag of sixteen tines, that they rode on their way through the forest to the castle of the earl of Caithness.

CHAPTER XVIII.

HOW THE TWO LADS HEARD OF THEIR MOTHER AGAIN.

NOTHING could they think of doing, when they came to their lodging, before they had out those old rags, their swaddling clothes. King Wiliam knew them at once, and said they were certainly his ; and both his sons fell upon him, clipping and kissing him again and again. He was quite as glad as they, and for reason. He kissed them and gave them joy, and blessed himself ; and such a to-do they made over it, that their host, the earl, came out with "Why, lads, have ye found a purse of gold ? "

"Never was a truer word, fair host ! " cried Wolfling. " A purse of gold ! Sir, a guest has come with us to your house, and no welcome is too good for him. Must I tell you all in a word ? It is the king of England ! Pray you, so please you, bid him in—your lord and ours. You will be fain of his friendship when he sits beside you in hall."

Wolfling began telling the earl all about it,

and he came forward eagerly, for he saw there were wonders afoot. The lads laid hold of their father by the hands, and dragged him forth to meet the earl, both at once telling the story, and their lord listened, and asked, until he had it all plainly set forth ; and then they showed him the proofs, the two rags of the king's robe, and he crossed himself and said there was never a doubt of the matter.

" You have met with a fine adventure," said he. " You have every right to be glad over it, though I fear me I shall be the loser for your rank which calls you to such higher service. There has never been any want of faith in you. If I made ye both my knights it was because ye were well worthy. Many a time and often you have served me right well in my wars. Many a time you have pricked the heart of that wicked proud lady yonder,—no peace to her yet till she wed me or yield to me ! "

" She will yield her lands to you to-morrow," said the king, " that I dare undertake. Never more need there be strife about that. If my two lads here have helped in your wars, out of thankfulness to a kind friend and foster, right and seemly it was, and no word have I against it. But if they had known who the lady was, woe betide them ! Sin and shame it is for a son to war upon his mother. Sin against God, crime against mankind, to prick her heart and give her grief. Mankind cries out upon it ; God loathes it. Nay, but such as these have sinned unwittingly ; ye never know the wrong ye did. For you it was right and good to help your lord in his quarrel : but ye must know this,—it was your mother ye have fought ; it was your mother's lands ye wasted and fired ; in that same act loyal to one law, disloyal to another. Both good and ill you did, and who am I to judge ? I can but say let us forgive and forget."

At this speech both Seaborn and Wolfling were sadly abashed, and whether for joy or grief the tears fell from their eyes.

" Good Lord in heaven ! " they cried, " when will it be day ? Oh, weary long it is before to-morrow comes. To-morrow morn we must go to our mother and pray her mercy for all that is past." And then they bethought them of the chapmen who had fostered them :—" They did so much more than they need, for they owed us nothing. It is but right they should see us again. Will they not be astonished when they know what their foundlings were? Oh, but they were very good to us."

In such talk one and the other held the earl of Caithness all that night. The servants made haste to dress a feast, and set it on the board, but morning was at hand before that supper ended.

CHAPTER XIX.

HOW THE QUEEN WENT TO THE RESCUE.

BUT from this merry feast we must go back to the poor queen, waiting in vain for her lord, and knowing at last that he was in the hands of her bitter foes. She made such weeping and wailing that she was like to die.

"Alas!" she said, "O evil tide! too short was my joy in him, and how much greater my grief for the little joy I had! Lord Jesus, why didst thou send me the bliss, to make the bale more bitter? Why didst thou give him back to me only to take him away? But I will not lose him! I will fight, I will save him,—or if they have slain him, this once they shall pay me dear. Up lords!" she cried, "and be doing! To-morrow we will fight them. Let cry through the land for all our power; bid them gather at break of day; let none bide at home, high or low, horse or foot, every soul who can bear spear or bow; and the ford shall be our trysting place."

Throughout all her lands they sent the cry that bade all to the hosting. Neither freeman nor thrall, as he loved his life, might gainsay it. Before hour of prime must every man tryst at the ford of the marches.

The next day at hour of prime came the queen to the host there gathered. Through the ford they passed, and never drew rein but rode on into the forest-land of Caithness.

In no great while they were aware of a company riding toward them, and soon made out the array of the earl. Nearer they came, and by now they could see the faces of those who rode over against them. What was the amazement of the queen when she knew her king in that array ! She pricked her horse, and galloped out ahead of her men ; and the king—he had no mind to cry out the news to her, but only signed his folk to halt, while he rode on, glad and happy, calling aloud, " Welcome, lady ! "

" Welcome, my dear lord, welcome too ! How did they take you ? Oh, tell me. Are you their prisoner or have they set you free ? If it is the ransom they seek, never trouble yourself, for here am I to pay it, if their folk will abide mine ! "

He laughed out, and turning to his two sons and the earl who had fostered them, " Ah, God in heaven ! " he cried, " May I not laugh ? Is not this a merry meeting ? Canst thou guess, dear sweetheart, what treasures I have found this voyage ? Indeed and truly, thine own gladness and mine I found even here on this spot yesterday. Well it was that I came hunting the stag of the sixteen tines ! Well found, well followed, well caught, well killed ! See, I have overcome thy foes ; they and their folk are here to cry pardon. Dost thou know these two who have wronged thee ? "

" I know who they must be, though I never saw them before. They must be those who have slain so many of my folk—who have harried and beaten me,—so raided my lands, and shorn my revenues, that outside city walls and fenced places they have left me nothing worth six silver shillings. Those were the first who came thinking to wed me to their lord. They were the kemps who took my men and held them to ransom. What more can I say? It is they who have made all this war—the cruellest, wickedest ruffians on this earth—who have so angered and tormented me that if there is one thing I know for a surety it is that yonder lads are my bitterest foes till death."

" And yet they are thy dearest friends by birth ! "

"Friends?" cried she. "How may that be?"

" Thy sons ! "

" God in heaven ! " she answered, " can that be so ? "

" Yes, and there is no doubt upon it."

He signed with his hand, and the companies of armed men closed up on either side, pressing round those two in their midst, and all full of wonder and eagerness for the tale there was to tell.

Never was there swifter step from hate to love. She could not doubt his word, and when she heard once more of her sons the yearning for them took her at the heart, and all woes and wrongs were forgotten in the gladness of that hour. She kissed them and clipped them in her arms, both at once, and yet said no word to them for sobbing at the joy that overcame her ; and they, who knelt low at her feet, amazed at their own happiness, blurted out their confession and prayer for pardon.

" Lady, forgive us if you can ! We have sinned, before heaven and in your sight. We know it now. We never knew it before. We thought it right. It was in ignorance we sinned : punish us as we deserve, but not more heavily."

"You have earned your pardon already," she answered. "After all, you meant to give me greater honour than I had! You thought me worthy of that, dear lads; never mind the rest!"

At this the earl of Caithness went over to her saying, "Lady, neither did I wrong you, in my heart I know it. Was it hate that made me beg your hand? I would have had you lady of all my lands; but when you scorned me, and when they told me you were thrall-born and base-bred, then indeed I was wrath, and gave you scorn for scorn. How should I know you were so far above me? Here I am then, to pray your forgiveness for all that is past."

"Sir earl, I am your debtor. I thank you heartily for my two sons : and with this first word of kindness you have won from me all that is in my power to give. All these lands which I have ruled so long I put into your hands—with my lord the king's leave."

"Leave!" said the king. "With my love and right good will; and still it seems far too little!"

So with all due form the lady of Sorlinc then and there made over her rights to the earl of Caithness ; and next without further delay they left the spot where such merry meetings had come about. The queen rode first, leading the two hosts now gladly foregathering, and nothing that gave her joy was any grief to them : there was never a soul on either side but was fain of her new-found happiness.

CHAPTER XX.

HOW THE CHAPMEN COME BACK INTO THE STORY.

SO they rode on their way to Sorlinc Castle and all in glee and gladness. But one thing was still wanting. Seaborn and Wolfling could not rest until they had sent for those chapmen their foster-fathers; and because there was none but was willing to have them brought to court, the lads made haste to send men on their errand.

The messengers looked high and low until they found the chapmen, and gave them so much of the tale as filled them with eagerness and delight. They came travelling day and night by the nearest way, and never left their rowing galley until they landed at Sorlinc, where the court was gathered. All the same, it was not the place where they would have chosen to be, and they wished it had been London or Winchester, York or Lincoln. Sorlinc haven was not beloved of merchantmen.

However, not to make a long story of it,

when they found that all the court was gathered there, they were well content. As they came up to the castle, Seaborn ran to meet them. Wolfling, who was a lad of ready wit, did his best to welcome them. They were brought straight before the king, who was all courtesy and kindness ; and Wolfling told the tale, and thought no shame in telling it.

" My lord, my lords, it is owing to these worthy men ye see before you that we are in the land of the living. This one saved me from the jaws of the wolf, and fostered me in his house. That one found Seaborn in the boat, and brought him up fair and fine. They gave us every kindness they could, and they have never had a single penny in reward of it. We have been a sheer loss to them. Now surely they ought to have some due return, and pray believe that anyone who loves them not can be no good friend of mine."

When he said that, the queen at once came forward and greeted the chapmen kindly. She took them aside out of the throng, and it seemed she would never tire of giving them joy and honour. First she bade fetch them fur mantles and greyskin cloaks that were hung up in her wardrobe. They thought themselves well paid, and were hugely pleased at these costly furs, which they said they could sell, and make heaps of money out of the bargain.

The queen laughed at that, and told them, " Nay, sirs, never fear ! I wish you to have these on the agreement that you wear them. You shall often have as good : these are only the arles I am giving you. You shall never want anything you will not get, never fear ! You need never go cheaping to fairs all the rest of your lives. I shall take good care that you and your kinsfolk are well off. You shall never lack silks nor purples, velvet nor vair, grey or sables, master Gonselin, nor you either, master Foukier ; for I hold you truly dear."

" But, lady, we are no fools, never think it ! If yon robes were ours, we could cut them up so cunningly that each would make fourteen pair of fine capes and trimmings ! "

" Oh, have done ! " said she, laughing, for she set very little store by her old furs.

" God's body, lady, we cannot take your robes. They are no use if we must not sell them ! "

How stupid these chapmen are, she thought, and laughed again. Why, if they are so silly as to set their hearts on selling the things, they shall. So she made them try on the robes, and when they were dressed, said she, " Now, sirs, sell me these gowns. I will buy them of you, but this is to be the bargain,—you must wear them afterwards."

They were both quite pleased, and said they would be glad to part with them for thirty marks, reckoning all in. " We could not take a farthing less," they said, " and that is the last word. No use trying to beat us down."

"God bless my soul!" said the lady. "Well, if you don't mind waiting a week or two."

So the bargain was made. They donned the costly robes, but so odd and queer they looked in them that anyone would think they were wearing borrowed plumes.

CHAPTER XXI.

HOW THE KING CAME TO HIS OWN AGAIN.

AT Sorlinc Castle the king of England stayed a week, and in that time the lands of Sorlinc were put into the hands of the earl of Caithness. Which done, without further delay, the ships were made ready in the harbour, and as there was nothing could tempt them to a longer sojourn there, they went aboard and set sail with a fair wind.

But Terfes was no longer shipmaster on that voyage. King William had not forgotten his friend, the chapman of Galloway, and had sent Terfes to bid him come to England. The chapman's two sons were already at court, and the king's word was pledged to them that they should find advancement and be made wardens of castles and peles.

The voyage was a fair one. This time the sea was calm, and a good wind with them, so that they failed not to make the haven of Yarmouth. As it hove in sight the king lifted up his voice and said, " Lord God, how swiftly come upon us either joy or grief, at the word of Thy will and ordinance! Oh God, surely never lived man on earth who bore such grief and trouble as I, nor had such joy and gladness as I have now!"

They landed and set out to find the rocks where the cave was,—Wolfling and Seaborn too, and master Foukier and master Gonselin, and the chapman's sons of Galloway, to whom both king and queen owed it to be more courteous and kindly than to all the rest; and indeed they gave them ample honour and friendliness.

When they came to the cave, king William took the earl of Caithness by the hand, saying to him, "Sir earl, look!—that is the bed. Oh, how well I recall it, how I mind me of the spot!—this is the chamber and that is the very bed where the queen lay with her two little babes. That way I ran after the wolf until I wearied out and fell. Yonder was Seaborn laid in the boat—behind there among the ships. It is so pleasant to be here once more, to think over all that befell me in this neighbourhood, the old sorrow and mishap now past and done with, that I cannot hasten away. Indeed I have no mind to thrust myself into any town, or even to knock at the gates of any castle of the realm until my nephew come and bid me welcome—for he is the king of the land, you know."

Near the cave they pitched their tents and settled for a while. But very soon the sound of their coming ran through the countryside, and king William's nephew hastened to meet him.

To London they all went with a great gathering, and folk were fain to see him, and greeted him gladly. There he stayed until his friend the chapman from Galloway came at his bidding ; and all people were told to serve and love him and honour him beyond any. The king himself, as well beseemed, loved him above all others. He made him his chief councillor, and his two sons he made knights and wedded them, the story tells, to the daughters of two wealthy earls, so that each of them was a lord in his own castle.

The young man who had sold him the horn at Bristol fair, and had given the money to the poor, was not forgotten. He was married to a very wealthy lady, and had a thousand marks a year. The two chapmen of Caithness also got a thousand sterling marks a year, and all lived happily ever afterwards.

But the king and his gentle lady and their two sons had so set their hearts upon the service of God that they won the joy He gives to those He loves. May that joy be yours who have heard to the end our tale of King William the Wanderer.

[THE END.]